Contents

How has shopping changed?

Many of the shops where we buy our food and other goods from today are very different from shops in the past.

Look at this **high street** in Nottingham 80 years ago. It had lots of small shops.

1928

Then and now

Look at the cars parked outside the shops and look on the next page at the shops today. Why are there no cars in the street any more?

Most shops sold a particular type of product, like books, shoes or hats.

Today there are fewer small shops in town centres. Look at Nottingham today.

The shops are a lot larger and sell more things. These large stores are often **chain stores**, which means they can be found in lots of different towns.

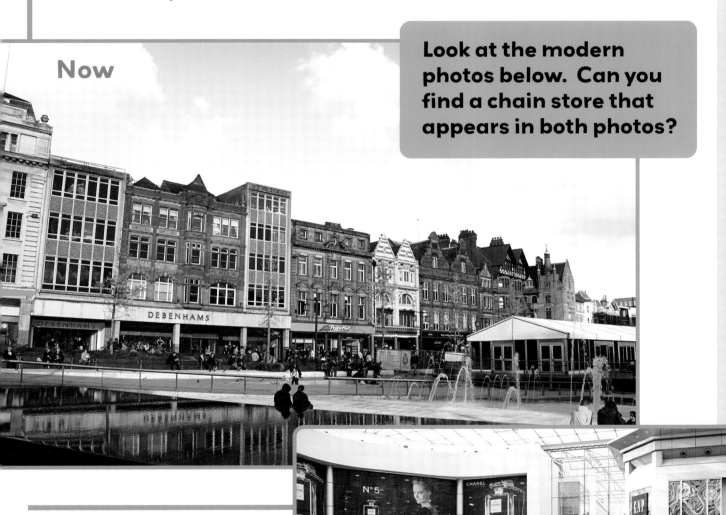

Now

Look at the modern photos below. Can you find a chain store that appears in both photos?

DEBENHAMS

Many towns now have indoor shopping centres, with lots of shops all in one huge building.

DEBENHAMS STYLING THE NATION

GAP

CHANEL

The marketplace

One of the earliest forms of shopping in towns was the open-air market. On market days, **traders** came and set up colourful stalls, each selling a particular type of product.

1933

In the 1930s the market was still a popular place to do your shopping. This is Banbury market in 1933. Most products on sale were locally produced.

Many towns still hold an open-air market. Markets may be held less often than in the past, but there are now more products for sale, like toys and electrical goods.

Look at the photo of Banbury market today.

Now

The fruit and vegetables may be grown at farms locally, but most market goods now come from other parts of the country or even from abroad.

Food shopping

If you did your food shopping a hundred years ago you would have to visit lots of different shops. Most towns and villages had a variety of small stores.

You would buy meat from a butcher's shop (right), bread from a bakery and fruit and vegetables from a greengrocers like the one below.

1900

A FLECKNELL

FRUIT & VEGETABLE MARK

FOR DISTINCTIVE MEN'S WEAR

1938

Shopping took a long time because you had to walk from one shop to the other.

How have things changed?
Shopping

First published in 2008 by
Franklin Watts
338 Euston Road
London NW1 3BH

Franklin Watts Australia
Level 17/207 Kent Street
Sydney NSW 2000

Copyright © Franklin Watts 2008

ISBN: 978 0 7496 7846 3

Dewey classification number: 381'.1

A CIP catalogue record for this book is available from the British Library.

Planning and production by Discovery Books Limited
Editor: James Nixon
Designer: Jill Jarrett

Photographs: p6 Courtesy of Nottingham City Council and www.picturethepast.org.uk, p7 Bobby Humphrey, p8 Getty Images, p9 Bobby Humphrey, p10 (top) Courtesy of Derbyshire Local Studies Libraries and www.picturethepast.org.uk, p10 (bottom) William H. Alden/Getty Images, p11 Chris Fairclough, p12 (top) Getty Images, p12 (bottom) Staffordshire Arts and Museum Service, p13 (top) Bobby Humphrey, p13 (bottom) Sainsbury's, p14 Maurice Ambler/Getty Images, p15 Chris Fairclough, p16 Bill Brandt/Getty Images, p17 Bobby Humphrey, p18 The Advertising Archives, p19 (bottom) The Advertising Archives, p20 (top) Courtesy of Derbyshire Local Studies Libraries and www.picturethepast.org.uk, p20 (bottom) Mary Evans Picture Library, p21 (top) Bobby Humphrey, p21 (bottom) Chris Fairclough, p22 Courtesy of Nottingham City Council and www.picturethepast.org.uk, p23 (top) Chris Fairclough, p23 (bottom) Sergey Kashkin/istockphoto.com, p24 (top) David Savill/GettyImages, p24 (bottom) Mary Evans Picture Library, p25 (top) Colin Woodbridge/ photographersdirect.com, p25 (bottom) Roger G. Howard/photographersdirect.com, p26 Mary Evans Picture Library, p27 (bottom) Bobby Humphrey.

Cover photos: (top) Maurice Ambler/GettyImages, (bottom) Chris Fairclough.

Printed in China

Franklin Watts is a division of Hachette Children's Books, an Hachette Livre UK company
www.hachettelivre.co.uk

Today we can do all of our food shopping under one roof in a supermarket. Supermarkets sell lots of other items as well as food, like clothes and **hardware.**

Find out for yourself

Visit the library and find pictures of shops in your town in the past. What kind of shops were there 50 years ago that have gone today? Have any shops stayed the same?

List the advantages and disadvantages of supermarkets.

There are now fewer small stores to be found in our towns. Some villages don't have any shops left at all.

11

Home deliveries

Before the 1950s most homes did not have a fridge for storing food, so lots of goods had to be bought fresh.

Families had to shop for a few items every day. This woman only needs a small hand basket to carry her shopping.

1925

1930

To help with the daily shopping, people had deliveries to their homes. This delivery truck is being loaded with **groceries**.

Most families now have fridges and freezers so foods like milk and meat can be kept for days or weeks. This means that we can do most of our food shopping in one weekly trip.

People can still have their shopping delivered. Supermarkets send their food to people's houses in vans like this one.

Service

Look at this grocery store from 1953. The shopkeeper stands behind the counter. Tins and cans are stacked high on the shelves behind him.

1953

Customers would ask the shopkeeper for everything they wanted and he would fetch it. You could talk to the shopkeeper or your friends while you queued to be served.

When we shop today we search the **aisles** ourselves for what we want. This is called self service.

Would shopping be quicker in the old or new store?

There are now a lot more products to choose from, but there is less chance to talk to the **checkout** operator or other people in the shop.

Packaging

In the 1940s fewer foods in shops were wrapped in plastic or paper packets. Many items were stored in bulk behind the counter in big bins.

The shopkeeper weighed the exact amount the customer wanted into paper bags.

This shopkeeper is weighing butter. It was weighed in pounds (about half a kilogram) and ounces (about 28 grams).

Nearly everything is packaged in today's supermarkets. Some items like sugar, butter and rice can be bought in different quantities, but they are nearly always in packets.

Then and now

Do you think it is better now that most foods are packaged? What problems can so much plastic packaging cause?

Even bigger items such as fruit and vegetables are often displayed in plastic packaging.

Adverts and money

Looking at old adverts is a good way of finding out how people spent their money in the past.

Look at this advert from 1954. Can you buy these sweets today?

Adverts looked quite different 50 years ago. They were usually drawn by an artist, like this poster for Rowntree's Fruit Gums.

Then

Money

Now

Before 1971 Britain used different money. Then there were coins like shillings, sixpences and florins.

Now look at this modern magazine advert. Like many adverts today it has been designed using photographs and a computer.

Then and now

Look at the cost of the sweets in the old and new adverts. The price 2d was about the same as 1p today. What would 1p buy you now?

Celebrities are now used in adverts to help sell a product. This Walkers crisps advert has the sports presenter Gary Lineker in it.

Clothes shopping

Most people could not afford to buy new clothes at the start of the twentieth century. Men might have owned one good suit, but in those days people would make their own clothes.

1899

Towns had a **draper's** shop like this one (right) where you could buy different materials.

1930

The materials came in all sorts of colours and patterns. The assistant would cut the **fabric** to the required length.

Today people can afford to spend money on new clothes more often. There are now a lot more clothes shops on the high street like this one.

Can you see the woman in the shop window? What do you think she is doing?

Most people no longer make their own clothes, but in some **communities** it is still common. This Muslim woman is selecting material from a modern fabric shop.

21

Retail parks

In the 1940s, shops selling large products, such as furniture or electrical goods, were located in shops or **department stores** in the high street.

1944

Most people did not have their own transport. Any large items bought then would usually have to be delivered to the customer's house.

By the 1950s most families had their own car. Town centres gradually got busier and parking became more difficult. Many shops that sold big items moved to **retail parks** on the outskirts of town where there was more space.

Can you think of some items people buy today that still have to be delivered to the home in a van, or lorry?

Now customers can park right outside the shop and load goods straight into the boot of the car. This customer has just bought some wood from the **DIY store.**

Street vendors

Goods were not always bought from shops or markets. It was common 70 years ago for street **vendors** to drive around and sell things.

1935

Ice cream sellers drove round on tricycles like this one. Bakers came round to sell cakes, too.

1940

This travelling salesman is selling all kinds of hardware from his lorry.

What can you see for sale on the lorry?

Street vendors selling from a van or truck are rarer today. But the jingle of the ice cream van is still a common sound in summer.

When was the last time you saw or heard an ice cream van? Do you remember where you were?

This ice cream van is not only selling lollies and ice cream. It is also towing a trailer full of beach toys for sale.

Mail-order shopping

There was another way to shop in the 1930s. Household goods and clothes could be ordered at home from a **catalogue** like this one.

Then and now

Compare the hats in the old and new catalogues. Do any of them look the same?

The product was then delivered to your door. This was an easier way to shop because it saved you time.

Today people still shop from catalogues. Look at the inside of this modern catalogue.

You can also order your shopping on the **Internet.** Since the invention of the World Wide Web in 1989 many more people now choose to shop from home.

Why is it helpful to order goods from the Internet? Do you prefer to shop at home or in the town?

People will still always want to go out and shop, however, because it is fun and you get to meet other people.

Glossary

Aisles The passages that run between the shelves in shops.

Catalogue A book listing things you can buy from a company.

Chain stores Shops that are found in a number of different towns.

Checkout The place in a shop where you pay for your goods.

Celebrities Famous people.

Communities Groups of people who live together in one area and share something in common with each other.

Customer A person who buys things from a shop or trader.

Department stores Large shops that sell a variety of goods in different departments.

DIY store DIY is an abbreviation for 'do it yourself'. DIY stores sell goods to people who are decorating or repairing things in their own home.

Draper A person who sells fabrics.

Fabric Any type of cloth.

Groceries Food and other household supplies.

Hardware Tools and other household equipment.

High street The main street of a town, traditionally the site for most shops.

Internet The worldwide computer network that allows information, such as a shopping order, to be exchanged from one person's computer to another.

Retail parks Shopping developments on the outskirts of town. They usually contain large chain stores.

Traders People who buy and sell goods.

Vendors People who are offering something for sale.

Further information

Places to visit:

Find out at the **local museum** or the **local library** the history of the shops in your town or village. You may find old photographs of the shops at these places.

How We Lived Then Museum of Shops, Eastbourne, East Sussex
(www.sussexmuseums.co.uk/how_we_lived_then.htm)
See a hundred years of shopping history in this museum's reconstructed old shops.

Milton Keynes Museum, Buckinghamshire (www.mkmuseum.org.uk)
This museum has recreated a typical Victorian street scene with street vendors and original shop fronts.

Brewhouse Yard Museum of Nottingham Life, Nottingham
(www.nottinghamcity.gov.uk/brewhouse_yard.htm)
There are numerous shops throughout the museum including an Edwardian grocery shop and a Victorian chemists.

Websites:

There are many websites where you can view historical photos of shops and shopping. Try the website of your **local council** and see if they have an image gallery.

www.gettyimages.com
has a large database of archive photos

www.staffspasttrack.org.uk
has historical images of Staffordshire shops

www.picturethepast.org.uk
for old photos of shops in the East Midlands

Books to read:

Changing Times: Shopping for Food, Ruth Thomson, 2004 (Franklin Watts)
Shopping in the 1940s, Faye Gardner, 2006 (Evans)
Where You Live: Going Shopping, Ruth Nason, 2007 (Franklin Watts)

Index